GIANT PANDAS

A TRUE BOOK

by

Patricia A. Fink Martin

Children's Press®
A Division of Scholastic Inc.

New York Toronto London Auckland Sydney
Mexico City New Delhi Hong Kong
Danbury, Connecticut

A panda feeds on bamboo.

Reading Consultant
Nanci R. Vargus, Ed.D.
*Primary Multiage Teacher
Decatur Township Schools,
Indianapolis, IN*

Content Consultant
Kathy Carlstead, Ph.D.
Honolulu Zoo

*Dedicated to my daughter,
Leslie Sara Martin*

*The photographs on the cover
and title page show giant
pandas in the bamboo forests
of China.*

Library of Congress Cataloging-in-Publication Data

Martin, Patricia A. Fink.
    Giant pandas / by Patricia A. Fink Martin.
        p. cm. — (A True book)
    Summary: Describes physical characteristics, behavior, habitat, and
endangered status of the giant panda
    ISBN 0-516-22165-5 (lib. bdg.)   0-516-27471-6 (pbk.)
    I. Giant panda—Juvenile literature. [1. Giant panda. 2. Pandas.
3. Endangered species.] I. Title. II. Series.
QL737.C214 M3387 2002
599.789—dc21   2001032300

1 2 3 4 5 6 7 8 9 10 R 11 10 09 08 07 06 05 04 03 02

Contents

Pandas live in the bamboo forests of China.

Animals of the Mountains

The giant panda is a mammal that lives high in the mountains of China. Forests with many tall trees cover the rocky mountain slopes. A tall, stiff grass called **bamboo** grows on the forest floor. These forests are the panda's home,

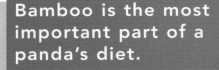

Bamboo is the most important part of a panda's diet.

and it feeds on bamboo there. The panda raises its young in tree hollows. Sometimes, it even climbs the big trees.

Giant pandas weigh between 200 and 300 pounds (90 to 135 kilograms) and stand on all four legs. If one stood next to you, it would only come up to your waist.

Pandas walk on all four legs.

Imagine touching a panda's fur. Its black and white coat may look soft, but the fur feels rough. An oily coating covers the stiff hairs. The oils keep the panda dry.

The panda's face is big and round, but it's not fat that makes it look chubby. Big muscles lie underneath its skin and fur. These muscles wrap from its jaws to the top of its head. These powerful muscles open and close its

A panda has a round face.

jaws. The panda needs these strong muscles to crunch bamboo stalks.

What Kind

Alaskan brown bear

Lions and leopards belong to the cat family. Wolves an[d] foxes are part of the dog family. But to what kind of family does the giant panda belong? In the past, scientists couldn't agree. Some scientists argued that the panda was a bear. It looks like a bear, and the two animal[s] blood is similar. Other scientists grouped

# of Animal?

the giant panda with the **red panda**, which belongs to the raccoon family. Both pandas live in China. Both eat bamboo. Both have big teeth for crushing stalks.

No one knows for sure where the panda belongs, but today most people agree that the giant panda is a bear.

Red panda

Champion Eaters

A panda spends a lot of time eating. It even gets up in the night to feed. It eats mostly bamboo. Because bamboo does not have many **nutrients**, the animal must eat a lot to become full.

The panda eats both the leaves and stems of the

A panda spends most of its day eating bamboo.

bamboo. But, the part it likes best is the young stems, or **shoots**. These shoots pop out of the ground in the spring.

What do bamboo shoots taste like? Try some and find out! You can find canned bamboo shoots in the grocery store. Ask your mother or father to buy them for you.

Bamboo shoots are soft and tender, but bamboo stems, or stalks, are woody and thick. The stems are

Bamboo leaves

A panda wraps its special thumb around a bamboo shoot.

therefore hard to eat and hard to hold. But the panda can do both easily. It does so by wrapping its curved fingers around a stem, and pressing the stem against its special thumb. The panda's thumb isn't like our thumb, however. It is made up of a bone in the panda's wrist.

The animal first bites off leaves with its teeth. Then it stuffs the leaves in its mouth. The panda uses its big back

A panda shows off its large teeth.

teeth to crack open a stem,
and then eats the soft inner
parts. A panda eats between
25 and 30 pounds (11 to 14 kg)
of stems and leaves a day.

A Panda's Day

A panda's day begins before the sun rises. It starts each day by looking for food, which is close by. A panda may only walk a mile (1.6 kilo-meters) or less in a day. It walks flat-footed, with its front feet pointed inward. The animal moves slowly on the ground. As it walks, its head swings from side to side. The giant panda eats bamboo either sitting or lying down. It eats all morning.

Sometimes a panda will lie on its back when it eats.

A panda naps during the day.

Later it might take a nap by leaning against a tree or boulder. Some pandas just curl up on the ground.

This panda (above) is drinking from a stream. A panda can climb into the treetops (right).

After the panda wakes, it may drink from a stream. Then it snacks on more bamboo. The panda may even take a swim or climb a tree. By late afternoon, it searches for food again. The panda eats for several hours. After the meal and a walk, the panda sleeps. It will sleep for only a few hours, because it will soon be hungry again.

Panda

Only a few scientists have traveled to the panda forests. They have found that wild pandas are hard to study. Pandas stay well hidden in the bamboo. As a result, scientists may only catch a quick look at them.

How do scientists study these secretive animals? First, they look for animal signs such as tracks. They also look for droppings. The droppings contain pieces of bamboo, which scientists measure

Scientists sometimes have to trap wild pandas.

Detectives

From the size of the pieces, they can learn the age and size of the animal.

Scientists sometimes trap a wild panda. Once it is caught, it is given a drug that makes it sleepy. While the animal sleeps, scientists weigh it and fit it with a special collar. When the panda wakes up, they release it.

The collar sends out signals that tell the scientists where the animal is. They can also tell if the panda is asleep or awake.

A special tracking collar is attached around the panda's neck.

Panda to Panda

Giant pandas live alone for most of their lives, and roam the forest by themselves. They search for the tastiest bamboo patches. Although they don't always return to the same place at night, they do have a home area or **territory**. Each panda stays in its own home area.

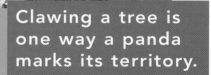

Clawing a tree is
one way a panda
marks its territory.

How does a panda know where other pandas live? The panda uses smells and signs to find other pandas. Under its tail is a special **gland**. This gland produces a smelly substance. Using its tail like a paintbrush, the panda paints the substance—and the smell—on trees and rocks. Pandas also scratch trees. The claw and scent marks send a message that tells other pandas to keep out.

A Panda Is Born

In the spring, male pandas look for mates. Female pandas leave special scent marks that help male pandas find them. Sometimes two or three male pandas show up. They roar and bark at each other. When the female is ready, she mates

Pandas look for mates in the spring.

with one of them. They stay together for only a short time.

By fall, the female panda is ready to have her cub. She has prepared a den in a cave or in a hollow tree. It is lined with

A newborn panda is very small.

twigs and leaves to provide a warm, safe place for the young cub.

One or two cubs may be born in the den. If two are

born, the mother panda raises only the strongest cub and leaves the other to die. A giant panda cub is the size of a hamster at birth. It has little hair on its body.

Baby pandas make a lot of noise.

rowing Up

The tiny panda cub squawks a lot. Its mother cuddles the cub in her paws and feeds it milk from her breasts.

Soon the cub grows fur and learns to crawl. In a few months, it trots beside its mother. Mother and cub are now able to leave the den

A mother panda cleans her cub.

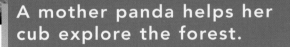

A mother panda helps her cub explore the forest.

together to feed. The cub begins to eat bamboo.

When the cub is one to two years old, it begins to wander. At first, the cub stays close to

Soon a cub learns to eat bamboo.

its mother's territory. Later, the young panda takes short trips alone, looking for its own place in the forest.

Endangered!

Once many giant pandas roamed across much of China. Today, only 1,200 pandas can be found in three small areas. Because there are so few left, they have been listed as an **endangered species**.

Even though Chinese laws protect the giant panda, some

People are
destroying
bamboo
forests.

people still hunt them. Their beautiful coats are worth a lot of money. Some pandas die in traps set for other animals.

The pandas are also losing their forest home. Farmers are clearing the forests to plant crops. Villagers are cutting down trees to use as firewood for cooking and heating their homes.

In some years, the panda can't find enough bamboo. Bamboo flowers once every

Bamboo
in bloom

Pandas need our help to survive.

ten to fifteen years. After that, the plant dies. A new plant grows from the seeds. But it takes time for a new plant to grow big and tall. During this time, many pandas cannot find food and starve to death.

You can help the pandas. You can read other books about them, or join a club that helps endangered animals. You can even raise money for their projects. Together, we can save these beautiful creatures.

To Find Out More

If you would like to learn more about giant pandas, check out these additional resources.

 **Books**

Dudley, Karen. **Giant Pandas.** Raintree Steck-Vaughn Publishers, 1997.

Helmer, Diana. **Panda Bears.** PowerKids Press, 1997.

Presnall, Judith. **The Giant Panda.** Lucent Books, 1998.

Tracqui, Valérie. **The Panda: Wild About Bamboo.** Charlesbridge Publishing, 1999.

Wexo, John Bonnett. **Pandas.** Zoobook Series, Wildlife Education, Ltd., 1998.

Willis, Terri Sichuan. **Panda Forests.** Raintree Steck-Vaughn Publishers, 1995.

Friends of the National Zoo
All About Pandas web site
http://www.fonz.org/ppage.htm

National Geographic Society
1145 17th Street, NW
Washington, DC
20036-4688
http://www.national geographic.com/kids/creature_feature/0011/pandas.html

San Diego Zoo, Giant Panda Research Station
P.O. Box 120551
San Diego, CA
92112-0551
http://www.sandiegozoo.org/special/pandas/index.html

Don't miss this great site. You can watch the pandas through the video cam!

Wildlife Conservation Society
2300 Southern Boulevard
Bronx, NY 10460
http://www.wcs.org

World Wildlife Fund
1250 24th Street, NW
Washington, DC 20037
http://www.wwf.org

Zoo Atlanta
Grant Park
800 Cherokee Avenue
Atlanta, GA 30315
http://www.zooatlanta.org

Visit this zoo to view two pandas on loan from China.

Important Words

bamboo a tall, stiff grass. In the United States, bamboo is often called cane.

endangered species a kind of living thing that is in danger of dying out

gland a body part that produces a fluid that is used by another part of the body

nutrient a substance needed by living things for growth and development

red panda a small mammal with red fur that resembles a raccoon. The red panda lives in China and eats bamboo leaves.

shoots the part of a plant that grows above ground. This usually refers to new plant growth in the spring.

territory the area in which an animal eats, sleeps, and does daily tasks. The animal will defend the area.

Index

Meet the Author

Patricia A. Fink Martin holds a doctorate in biology. After spending many years teaching and working in the laboratory, she began writing science books for children. In 1998, *Booklist* chose her first book, *Animals that Walk on Water*, as one of the ten best animal books for children for that year. She has since published eight more books. Dr. Martin lives in Tennessee with her husband Jerry, their daughter Leslie, and their golden retriever Ginger.